W9-CES-579

Watchmen on the Walls

PRAYING

CHARACTER

INTO YOUR

CHILD

Watchmen on the Walls

ANNE ARKINS & GARY HARRELL

Multnomah Publishers *Sisters, Oregon*

WATCHMEN ON THE WALLS
published by Multnomah Publishers, Inc.

and in association with FamilyLife, a division of Campus Crusade for Christ

© 1995, 1996 by FamilyLife
International Standard Book Number: 1-57673-373-4

Cover photograph © 1998 by Joe Cornish/Tony Stone Images

Scripture quotations are from:
New American Standard Bible (NASB) © 1960, 1977 by the Lockman Foundation

The Holy Bible, New International Version (NIV)
© 1973, 1984 by International Bible Society,
used by permission of Zondervan Publishing House

The Amplified Bible (AMP) © 1965, 1987 by Zondervan Publishing House.
The Amplified New Testament © 1958, 1987 by the Lockman Foundation.

The Living Bible (TLB) © 1971. Used by permission of Tyndale House Publishers, Inc.
All rights reserved.

The Everyday Bible, New Century Version (NCV)
© 1987 by Worthy Publishing, used by permission.

The New Testament in Modern English, Revised Edition (Phillips)
© 1958, 1960, 1972 by J. B. Phillips

Printed in the United States of America

For information:
MULTNOMAH PUBLISHERS, INC.
POST OFFICE BOX 1720
SISTERS, OREGON 97759

98 99 00 01 02 03 04 — 10 9 8 7 6 5 4 3 2 1

TABLE OF CONTENTS

PREFACE

This book was born out of frustration...the frustration that comes from desiring to reach into our children's lives through prayer and touch places that are far beyond our control. We knew that prayer worked, but at the same time we experienced prayer that became superficial and routine. Too often we heard ourselves say, "Dear God, bless our children." It was our desire to go deeper, to claim the varied and rich promises contained in God's Word, and to literally pray these promises into the lives of our children.

Two basic convictions form the foundation for this work. First of all, *our children, created in the image of God, are worthy of the sacrifices demanded by faithful and consistent prayer.* There are many times as a parent when far greater results come from quiet communion with our God than from all the rhetoric available to man.

Second, *prayer changes things.* John Wesley said, "God will do nothing but in answer to prayer." S.D. Gordon said, "The greatest thing anyone can do for God and for man is to pray." Likewise, E.M. Bounds states, "God shapes the world by prayer. The more praying there is in the world the better the world will be, the mightier the forces against evil." With these convictions we also desire to move, shape, and fashion the very hearts of our children through prayer.

As for a guiding verse, perhaps no portion of Scripture captures our hearts' desire more than Isaiah 62:6-7. The Living Bible version reads, "O Jerusalem, I have set intercessors on your walls who shall cry to God all day and all night for the fulfillment of His promises. Take no rest, all you who pray, and give God no rest until He establishes Jerusalem and makes her respected and admired throughout the earth." Is God concerned only for a city of brick and mortar? No, His heart is for the people who make up that city.

We can pray aggressively, calling out to God and "giving Him no rest" until He fulfills the promises He has already graciously given in His Word.

May we truly become faithful "watchmen on the walls" as we pray for our children—that they become young men and young women full of the Word and mighty in His Spirit.

A NOTE TO OUR READERS

As writers, we face a dilemma. The English language does not contain a one-word equivalent for "he or she," yet we find it cumbersome to repeatedly refer to your child as "he or she." Therefore, for the sake of readability, we generally will refer to your child as "he."

HOW TO USE THIS PRAYER GUIDE

Our purpose for this book is to help you pray systematically and specifically for character traits to be built into your child's life. We've chosen 12 traits and devoted five days to each.

For each day, you will find a promise from Scripture and a suggested prayer. You might want to use our prayer as a starting point, as well as pray for specific needs in your child's life.

At the end of each section, you will find "action steps" that will help you teach your child the character trait for which you have prayed. Feel the freedom to use these suggestions as they apply to your child. As you pray for your child, God may impress upon you action steps more specific to your child. If you cannot implement an action step, you might pass the idea on to someone else.

Finally, use the "prayer journal" page at the end of each character trait to record current circumstances, feelings, and prayers concerning your child. Return to that page later and record how you've seen God answers your prayers in the life of your child.

Our hope is that this book is the tool that helps you to regularly and continually speak with the Father about your concerns for your child.

"Those who always pray are necessary to those who never pray."

—VICTOR HUGO

Day 1

Kindness is giving up something for the benefit of another.

"The Samaritan went to him and poured olive oil and wine on his wounds and bandaged them. He put the hurt man on his own donkey and took him to an inn. At the inn, the Samaritan took care of him. The next day, the Samaritan brought out two silver coins and gave them to the innkeeper. The Samaritan said, 'Take care of this man. If you spend more money on him, I will pay it back to you when I come again.'"

–Luke 10:34-35 (NCV)

PRAYER FOCUS:
Father, may _____ be willing to give of himself to help a person in need. May _____ not only see the needs of others but act upon these needs in a sacrificial way. Deliver _____ from holding too tightly to his own possessions. Give him a willingness to share what he has with others.

This is how we know what real love is: Jesus gave his life for us. So we should give our lives for our brothers. Suppose a believer is rich enough to have all that he needs. He sees his brother in Christ who is poor and does not have what he needs. What if the believer does not help the poor brother? Then the believer does not have God's love in his heart. My children, our love should not be only words and talk. Our love must be true love. And we should show that love by what we do.

–1 John 3:16-18 (NCV)

PRAYER FOCUS:
Gracious Father, open _____'s heart to know the real love of Jesus' gift of salvation. Help him be willing to give of himself for others. May _____ be sensitive to see ways he can meet the needs of the people around him. Father, help _____ to love others not only in words.

Day 2

Kindness is having a sensitive spirit toward others.

It is a sin to hate your neighbor. But being kind to the needy brings happiness.

–Proverbs 14:21 (NCV)

PRAYER FOCUS:
Father, as _____ sees those around him in need (physical, emotional, or spiritual need), may his heart be touched. Give him a desire to help them. May _____ realize that it is a sin to hate his neighbor, but being kind to those in need will bring him happiness.

...I taught you to remember the words of Jesus. He said, "It is more blessed to give than to receive."

–Acts 20:35b (NCV)

PRAYER FOCUS:
Lord Jesus, may _____ recognize the value of being kind. I pray that _____ will experience the blessing that comes with giving.

A gentle answer will calm a person's anger. But an unkind answer will cause more anger.

–Proverbs 15:1 (NCV)

PRAYER FOCUS:
Gentle Father, cause _____ to learn to respond to the anger of another with a gentle answer. Open the eyes of _____ to see that the gentleness and kindness of speech can do far more than an unkind word to stop another person's anger.

Day 3

Kindness is treating others the way we would like to be treated.

Do not mistreat foreigners (new people) living in your country. Treat them just as you treat your own citizens. Love foreigners as you love yourselves, because you were foreigners one time....

–Leviticus 19:33-34a (NCV)

P R A Y E R   F O C U S :

Loving Father, as _____ comes in contact with new people in his life, may he treat them as he would a friend. Help _____ to love, accept, and show compassion for the people he encounters.

———————————

"Do for other people what you want them to do for you."

–Luke 6:31 (NCV)

P R A Y E R   F O C U S :

Lord, develop in _____ a willingness to do for others what he would like others to do for him.

———————————

"I was hungry, and you gave me food. I was thirsty, and you gave me something to drink. I was alone and away from home, and you invited me into your house. I was without clothes, and you gave me something to wear. I was sick, and you cared for me. I was in prison, and you visited me."

–Matthew 25:35-36 (NCV)

P R A Y E R   F O C U S :

Lord Jesus, I pray that _____ will learn to look at the needs of others with mercy and tenderness. Encourage _____ to become a lifeline to those around him who need a meal or even a drink of water; those who may need a friend or even a smile.

Day 4

Kindness is controlling our negative thoughts toward others.

Do not be bitter or angry or mad. Never shout angrily or say things to hurt others. Never do anything evil. Be kind and loving to each other. Forgive each other just as God forgave you in Christ.

–Ephesians 4:31-32   (NCV)

P R A Y E R   F O C U S :

Loving, gracious Father, help _____ to resolve his conflicts instead of harboring bitterness or anger in his heart. May he never shout angrily or say things to hurt others. I pray that _____ will not do evil things but will be kind and loving. Give _____ the desire to forgive just as You have forgiven him in Christ.

_____

Then Joseph said to them, "Don't be afraid. Can I do what only God can do? You meant to hurt me. But God turned your evil into good. It was to save the lives of many people. And it is being done. So don't be afraid. I will take care of you and your children." So Joseph comforted his brothers and spoke kind words to them.

–Genesis 50:19-21   (NCV)

P R A Y E R   F O C U S :

Father, I pray that _____ may become sensitive to Your control of the events and people in his life. Show _____, like Joseph, how to handle the negative thoughts he has toward others, especially those people who have caused him pain or offended him.

Day 5

Selfishness is acting according to one's own interests and needs without regard for the needs of others.

For people will love only themselves and their money; they will be proud and boastful, sneering at God, disobedient to their parents, ungrateful to them, and thoroughly bad. They will be hardheaded and never give in to others;...

–2 Timothy 3:2-3a (TLB)

P R A Y E R   F O C U S :
O Lord, guard the heart of my child from the error of selfishness. I earnestly pray that _____ would not be caught up in thinking only of himself and his needs. Keep _____ from being proud and boastful, disregarding You, disobeying us as his parents, and forgetting to be grateful. Cause _____ to recognize selfishness in his life and confess it to You.

"For everyone who exalts himself shall be humbled, and he who humbles himself shall be exalted."

–Luke 14:11 (NASB)

P R A Y E R   F O C U S :
Father, deliver _____ from any attitude of self-exaltation. Grant _____ a willingness and eagerness to be humble before You and before others. Refocus the vision of _____'s selfishness, so that he can see the needs of others and what's best for them.

ACTION STEPS:

1. Read the passage on Joseph and ask your son or daughter to relate their feelings about how Joseph responded to his brothers. Help them to see how Joseph's character quality of kindness ultimately showed his faith in God's control...not other people.

2. Draw a name at each meal time this week, and share a kind word of encouragement and appreciation about the person whose name was drawn.

3. Ask each family member to consider what they might give up this week that would benefit someone less fortunate than themselves. Make plans to share at the end of the week the blessings everyone received as they gave.

4. Select, at random, secret pals within your family. Set specific time and money limits, and do kind deeds for your secret pal.

HUMILITY

*"The greatest thing
anyone can do for God
and man is pray."*

—S. D. GORDON

Day 1

Humility is thinking more highly of others than you do of yourself.

Do nothing out of selfish ambition or vain conceit, but in humility consider others better than yourselves. Each of you should look not only to your own interests, but also to the interests of others.

–Philippians 2:3-4 (NIV)

P R A Y E R   F O C U S :
Merciful God, You allowed Your only Son to humble Himself and become our servant. He did nothing out of selfish ambition or self-importance. May _____ likewise humbly consider others to be better than himself. Give _____ the sensitivity to see beyond his own interests to what is important for those around him.

———————

Be devoted to one another in brotherly love. Honor one another above yourselves.

–Romans 12:10 (NIV)

P R A Y E R   F O C U S :
O Lord, develop in _____ a real willingness to become devoted to others in brotherly love. Liberate _____ to see the importance of putting others before himself in his life.

Day 2

Humility is developing spiritual greatness through servitude.

"The greatest among you will be your servant. For whoever exalts himself will be humbled, and whoever humbles himself will be exalted."
—Matthew 23:11-12 (NIV)

P R A Y E R   F O C U S :
Lord, it's a hard thing to learn how to put others above yourself and serve them with a willing heart in true humility. Create in _____ 's heart a receptiveness to the opportunities in his life that help him to apply this principle. Reveal to _____ that real character is being able to humble himself before You and others.

"But you are not to be like that. Instead, the greatest among you should be like the youngest, and the one who rules like the one who serves."
—Luke 22:26 (NIV)

P R A Y E R   F O C U S :
Father, allow _____ to catch a vision of what Christ means when He says the greatest is like the youngest and the one who rules like the one who serves. May he desire to develop this attitude in his own life and recognize ways he can grow in this regard.

Day 3

Humility puts our children in a position to receive the refreshing grace of God.

The high and lofty one who inhabits eternity, the Holy One, says this: I live in that high and holy place where those with contrite, humble spirits dwell; and I refresh the humble and give new courage to those with repentant hearts.
–Isaiah 57:15 (TLB)

P R A Y E R   F O C U S :
Lord God, You alone are the high and lofty One. Give _____ a humble attitude before You. May he have a repentant spirit and be receptive to Your Spirit dwelling in him.

———————————

...Scripture says: "God opposes the proud but gives grace to the humble."...Humble yourselves before the Lord, and He will lift you up.
–James 4:6b, 10 (NIV)

P R A Y E R   F O C U S :
Father, You are the one who exalts Your children. I ask that You would lift up _____ as he humbles himself before You. Give him eyes to see the destructiveness of pride, and may _____ learn that humbly yielding to Your Lordship allows him to receive Your power.

Day 4

Humility is having a correct evaluation of ourselves.

...I, by the grace God gave me, give this advice to each one of you. Don't cherish exaggerated ideas of yourself or your importance, but try to have a sane estimate of your capabilities....

–Romans 12:3a (Phillips)

PRAYER FOCUS:
Lord Jesus, You are the perfect God. I earnestly ask that _____ will not have an attitude of superiority or perfectionism. Please allow _____ to see himself as one of Your wonderfully gifted creations. Grant him clear and correct insight into the capabilities You have given him.

Work happily together. Don't try to act big. Don't try to get into the good graces of important people, but enjoy the company of ordinary folks. And don't think you know it all!

–Romans 12:16 (TLB)

PRAYER FOCUS:
Father, thank you that You free us to enjoy people of every status. I ask that You give _____ the gift of humility. Supply _____ with a correct evaluation of himself in regard to those with whom he will work and play. May he not have a know-it-all attitude.

Day 5

Pride leads to an incorrect estimation of oneself in relation to others.

For we are not bold to class or compare ourselves with some of those who commend themselves; but when they measure themselves by themselves, and compare themselves with themselves, they are without understanding.
                                                        –2 Corinthians 10:12 (NASB)

PRAYER FOCUS :
Father, though You are exalted, You regard the lowly. I humbly pray that _____ would be one of those who correctly evaluates himself. Keep _____ from falling into the trap of comparing himself with others.

_____

For if any person thinks himself to be somebody [too important to condescend to shoulder another's load], when he is nobody [of superiority except in his own estimation], he deceives and deludes and cheats himself.
                                                        –Galatians 6:3 (AMP)

PRAYER FOCUS :
Lord God, I ask that You might take away from _____ any arrogant attitude of superiority. I pray that _____ would not believe the lie, "I have to be 'somebody' to be important." Entrust _____ with a spirit of humility that is willing to meet another's need.

A C T I O N   S T E P S :

1. Spend time one evening brainstorming the idea of humility. Then ask family members to write out one way they could actually apply humility in regard to their family this week. Set a time to get back together and discuss the results.

2. Share with your child one of the interesting phenomena of nature we've learned from observing wildlife: When two mountain goats meet on a steep and narrow mountain ledge, one of them will lie down and allow the other to walk on top of him so they can pass. Talk about the ways "humility" lies down before others in the everyday confrontations of life.

"I have been driven many times to my knees by the over-whelming conviction that I had nowhere else to go."

—ABRAHAM LINCOLN

Day 1

Teachability is developing a heart-attitude that seeks God's guidance for living to honor Him each day.

Teach me to do your will, for you are my God; may your good Spirit lead me on level ground.

–Psalm 143:10 (NIV)

P R A Y E R   F O C U S :
Almighty God, how thankful I am that I can bring _____ to You in prayer. Look lovingly upon him, and teach _____ to do Your will because You are his God. Allow Your Spirit to lead him on level ground. Lord, guide _____ in the path he goes today that it would be the direction You would choose for him.

_____

...guide me in your truth and teach me, for you are God my Savior, and my hope is in you all day long.

–Psalm 25:5b (NIV)

P R A Y E R   F O C U S :
God and Savior, You alone are able to guide my child in the right path. I place _____ in Your loving care. I ask that You would instruct him in Your truth and teach him Your way. May _____ 's hope be in You each and every day of his life.

Day 2

Teachability helps our children prepare their hearts to be faithful to God.

Then they would put their trust in God and would not forget his deeds but would keep his commands. They would not be like their forefathers—a stubborn and rebellious generation, whose hearts were not loyal to God, whose spirits were not faithful to him.

–Psalm 78:7-8 (NIV)

P R A Y E R   F O C U S :
Father, it is Your own Spirit that teaches us through Your Word. I pray _____ will yield to Your instruction. Please protect _____ from developing a stubborn or rebellious spirit. May he be a spiritual sponge, soaking up Your truth.

———————————

But Daniel resolved not to defile himself with the royal food and wine, and he asked the chief official for permission not to defile himself this way.

–Daniel 1:8 (NIV)

P R A Y E R   F O C U S :
Lord, You alone know the circumstances my child will face on any given day. I lift _____ before You and pray that he begins preparing his heart to be faithful to You alone—no matter what circumstances he finds himself to be in. Father, begin to develop in _____ the courage and conviction to be a Daniel in his generation.

Day 3

Teachability is having a mind that seeks truth and having ears that are sensitive and willing to hear knowledge and rebuke.

The mind of the prudent is ever getting knowledge, and the ear of the wise is ever seeking—inquiring for and craving—knowledge.

–Proverbs 18:15 (AMP)

PRAYER FOCUS:
Father, I ask You for a teachable heart and an attentive attitude in
_____. Open his mind to the truth of Your Word, and make his ears sensitive to the godly wisdom of others.

Like an earring of gold or an ornament of fine gold is a wise man's rebuke to a listening ear.

–Proverbs 25:12 (NIV)

PRAYER FOCUS:
Lord, You are the Great Teacher. I pray that my child might have a wise and listening ear. Train _____ to be open to loving rebuke.

Day 4

Teachability is allowing ourselves to be instructed by the Lord.

Every young man who listens to me and obeys my instructions will be given wisdom and good sense....For wisdom and truth will enter the very center of your being, filling your life with joy.

–Proverbs 2:1, 10 (TLB)

P R A Y E R   F O C U S :
Father, You are the Giver of every good and perfect gift. Thank You that You want to give wisdom and instruction to my child. Lord, I desire that the very center of _____ 's being be like a dry sponge to soak up Your sweet and refreshing teachings.

Thus says the Lord, "Let not a wise man boast of his wisdom, and let not the mighty man boast of his might, let not a rich man boast of his riches; but let him who boasts boast of this, that he understands and knows Me,..."

–Jeremiah 9:23-24a (NASB)

P R A Y E R   F O C U S :
God, You are the deep spring of all wisdom and knowledge that flows to us daily. I humbly ask that _____ will not boast in his own wisdom but will allow himself to be instructed in life by You, the Giver of life. Grant him a teachable spirit.

Day 5

Stubbornness is changing only under the pressure of negative circumstances.

Do not be as the horse or as the mule which have no understanding, whose trappings include bit and bridle to hold them in check, otherwise they will not come near to you.

–Psalm 32:9 (NASB)

PRAYER FOCUS:
God of truth, deliver _____ from being a stubborn child. As he passes through each stage of life may he learn to yield to those circumstances of life that You use to guide him into righteousness.

———————————

The man who is often reproved but refuses to accept criticism will suddenly be broken and never have another chance.

–Proverbs 29:1 (TLB)

PRAYER FOCUS:
Father, it is my request that _____ be a child that is quick to accept criticism and to learn and grow from it. My prayer is for _____ to never have to be broken by You because of his stubbornness.

A C T I O N S T E P S :

1. To stimulate mealtime conversation, discuss the following questions:

    a. What are the characteristics of a teachable person?
    b. Why it is difficult to listen to and accept the rebuke of another?

2. Discuss who is the most teachable person...

    a. In the Bible
    b. In your family
    c. You've ever known

3. As a fun family project, take one evening to explore what it means to be teachable. Use Dad to model this attitude. Share some changes you would like for him to make...but he must have his mouth taped shut. This is an important (and fun) visual reminder that a teachable person does not give excuses.

"Intercession is basically love praying. In the very truest sense, intercession is love on its knees."

—DICK EASTMAN

Day 1

**Forgiveness is God's gift to us through the death and resurrection
of Jesus Christ. It allows us to have new life
and eternal fellowship with God.**

*In Christ we are set free by the blood of His death. And so we have
forgiveness of sins because of God's rich grace.*

–Ephesians 1:7 (NCV)

PRAYER FOCUS:
Gracious Father, we thank You that _____ is/or can be set free by the
blood of Christ's death. May _____ understand that he has forgiveness
of sins because of Your rich grace.

_____

*Where is another God like you, who pardons the sins of the survivors among
his people? You cannot stay angry with your people, for you love to be
merciful. Once again you will have compassion on us. You will tread our
sins beneath your feet; you will throw them into the depths of the ocean!*

–Micah 7:18-19 (TLB)

PRAYER FOCUS:
Father, I thank You for being such a merciful God. Help _____ not be
hesitant in coming to You in confession and repentance. Touch _____'s
heart with the understanding of how completely You forgive when he
repents of his sin and returns to You.

Day 2

Forgiveness frees from a judgmental and critical spirit.

"And do not judge and you will not be judged; and do not condemn, and you will not be condemned; pardon, and you will be pardoned."

–Luke 6:37   (NASB)

P R A Y E R   F O C U S :
Father, give _____ a forgiving spirit. Help him to not look upon the weaknesses of others. Give _____ the strength to give up any resentment he is harboring that can grow out of a failure to forgive others.

―――――――――――

"And even if he sins against you seven times in a day, and turns to you seven times and says, 'I repent' (I am sorry), you must forgive him—[that is,] give up resentment and consider the offense as recalled and annulled."

–Luke 17:4   (AMP)

P R A Y E R   F O C U S :
Father, help _____ endure in forgiveness and repeatedly forgive those that fail him and You. Guard _____ from becoming critical and judgmental when he is faced with the weaker habits of others.

Day 3

Forgiveness is responding to evil by doing good.

Never pay back evil for evil. Do things in such a way that everyone can see you are honest clear through. Don't quarrel with anyone. Be at peace with everyone, just as much as possible. Dear friends, never avenge yourselves. Leave that to God, for He has said that He will repay those who deserve it.
                                                        —Romans 12:17-19 (TLB)

P R A Y E R   F O C U S :
Dear God, I pray that _____ will be willing to learn not to repay evil for evil. Help him to learn what true love is—the love that Christ has for us. Teach _____ that he must not try to get even, but leave that up to You. Lord, help _____ see that forgiveness can break the "getting back at others" cycle and bring healing to relationships. And may _____ discover how right actions can lead to right attitudes.

_____

People insulted Christ, but he did not insult them in return. Christ suffered, but he did not threaten. He let God take care of him. God is the One who judges rightly.

                                                        —1 Peter 2:23 (NCV)

P R A Y E R   F O C U S :
Dear God, thank You for sending Your Son to be the ultimate example of forgiveness. May _____ be willing to love others and forgive them in spite of their wrong ways. Help him see that turning away from a tough situation can be used to soften hearts.

Day 4

Forgiveness is the gift we must receive in order to forgive others.

"And forgive our sins—for we have forgiven those who sinned against us...."
–Luke 11:4a (TLB)

P R A Y E R   F O C U S :
Dear Father, speak to _____ 's heart about forgiveness. Help him see the need to receive Your forgiveness for his sin. May _____ then see the need to forgive those who have wronged or offended him.

_____

"But when you are praying, first forgive anyone you are holding a grudge against, so that your Father in heaven will forgive you your sins too."
–Mark 11:25 (TLB)

P R A Y E R   F O C U S :
Lord, I know Your desire is to forgive _____ when he is separated from You by sin in his life. I truly pray that he will not be a person who holds grudges but will quickly and joyfully forgive others.

Day 5

Revenge is the act of inflicting punishment or injury in return for what one has suffered at the hand of another.

Do not do wrong to a person to pay him back for doing wrong to you. Or do not insult someone to pay him back for insulting you. But ask God to bless that person....

–1 Peter 3:9a   (NCV)

P R A Y E R   F O C U S :
Almighty God, You alone have the right to repay evil that is done to us by others. May _____ accept this as Your justice and choose not to show revenge for the wrong done to him by others. In turn, help _____ to give a blessing instead, that others will know _____ is Yours.

Most importantly, love each other deeply. Love has a way of not looking at others' sin.

–1 Peter 4:8   (NCV)

P R A Y E R   F O C U S :
Father, I pray that _____ would come to recognize the deep need to not retaliate in revenge but to forgive those who offend him. Release him from any sense of revenge in his life. May _____'s eyes be on Jesus Christ and not the insults of others. Lord, bring to _____'s mind his own weaknesses so that he might have compassion for the weaknesses of others. Help him to see that love covers a multitude of sins.

A C T I O N S T E P S :

1. Have someone read aloud Matthew 7:3 (NASB).
Bring a moderate-sized log from the wood pile and place
it at different spots around the house on consecutive
days—reminding everyone daily to forgive others and get
the log out of our own eyes before we try to critically get
the speck out of someone else's eye.

2. Suggest that each family member spend 10-15 minutes
alone this evening making a list of sins they have not
confessed or people they have not forgiven. Then have
each person write out 1 John 1:9 over this list. Lay these
at the foot of the cross in prayer, and destroy the list.
Then thank God for His forgiveness!

3. Parent, look for an opportunity this week to encourage
your child in this area. Be aware of any situations where
Luke 17:4 might be applied and discussed with the child.
For example, who are some specific people in your child's
life you can encourage him to reach out to with love and
forgiveness rather than respond to with bitterness and
revenge?

"The force of prayer is greater than any possible combination of man-controlled powers, because prayer is man's greatest means of trapping the infinite resources of God."

—J. EDGAR HOOVER

Day 1

**Obedience puts children in proper relation to their parents—
God's representative authorities.**

*Children, obey your parents in the Lord [as His representatives], for this is just
and right. Honor (esteem and value as precious) your father and your
mother;...*

–Ephesians 6:1-2a (AMP)

P R A Y E R   F O C U S :
Lord, I ask that _____ willingly and eagerly obeys us as his parents.
Allow him to recognize and accept joyfully the fact that we are Your
representatives to guide and direct him—and Father, please give us as
_____ 's parents, wisdom. We want to be valued as precious
by_____.

---

*And He went down with them and came to Nazareth, and was (habitually)
obedient to them;...And Jesus increased in wisdom (in broad and full
understanding), and in stature and years, and in favor with God and man.*

–Luke 2:51a-52 (AMP)

P R A Y E R   F O C U S :
Dear God, I pray that _____ becomes consistently obedient in every
area of his life. Cultivate in him the desire to develop godly habits
through obedience to the Word of God.

Day 2

Obedience puts children in proper relation to the outside authorities in their lives—teachers, church leaders, police, etc.

Let every person be loyally subject to the governing (civil) authorities. For there is no authority except from God—by His permission,...

—Romans 13:1a (AMP)

P R A Y E R   F O C U S :
Father, impart to _____ the willingness to be submissive to the many governing and ruling authorities in our country. Develop in _____ a deep respect for the laws of our land and for those who enforce them, a mind for Your thoughts, and a desire to be active in the development of our country.

_____

Remind people to be submissive to [their] magistrates and authorities, to be obedient,...and to show unqualified courtesy toward everybody.

—Titus 3:1a, 2b (AMP)

P R A Y E R   F O C U S :
Father, may Your Holy Spirit remind _____ to be submissive to his teachers in school and in church. Convey to _____ the need to show them courtesy and respect by being quick to do what he is told.

Day 3

Obedience is a heart attitude that should characterize the spirit of my child; it is not just an outward act.

...God sees not as man sees, for man looks at the outward appearance, but the Lord looks at the heart.

−1 Samuel 16:7b (NASB)

P R A Y E R   F O C U S :
Lord, I want to thank You and trust You for a child that is obedient in his behavior. Lord, I pray that Your Holy Spirit might drive deeper into _____ 's soul an attitude and spirit of obedience. Give _____ the understanding that You see the things he does in secret and that You even know his innermost thoughts.

...what does the Lord your God require of you, but (reverently) to fear the Lord your God: [that is,] to walk in all His ways, and to love Him, and to serve the Lord your God with all your [mind and] heart and with your entire being,...

−Deuteronomy 10:12 (AMP)

P R A Y E R   F O C U S :
Father, instill in _____ a desire to obey You. I ask that his obedience to me be not because I'm the parent, but because You have put within him a reverence for You and for Your Word.

Day 4

Obedience puts material things into proper perspective, and shields our children from the dangers of peer pressure.

"No one can serve (obey) two masters. Either he will hate the one and love the other, or he will be devoted to the one and despise the other. You cannot serve (obey) both God and Money."

–Matthew 6:24 (NIV)

P R A Y E R   F O C U S :
Heavenly Father, I would ask You to save _____ from the trap of letting his life be spent desiring and pursuing material possessions. Fill his mind with Your thoughts instead of the things that are constantly fed into his mind. Allow him to find that inner beauty and strength that comes from obeying You, not from gaining material possessions.

But if you are unwilling to obey the Lord, then decide today whom you will obey....But as for me and my family, we will serve the Lord.

–Joshua 24:15 (TLB)

P R A Y E R   F O C U S :
Lord, cause _____ to see that although many people choose not to obey You, he must make his own commitment. Give him the strength to uphold his commitment to You even when it gets tough. Father, may _____'s own resolve to obey You be a shield and protection from the forces that would desire to press him into the world's mold.

Day 5

Disobedience is willfully choosing not to follow a command or law.

"Don't be frightened," Samuel reassured them. "You have certainly done wrong, but make sure now that you worship the Lord with true enthusiasm, and that you don't turn your back on him in any way."

–1 Samuel 12:20 (TLB)

P R A Y E R   F O C U S :
O Lord, thank You for Your mercy even when we disobey. I ask that
_____ would see clearly when he is wrong and disobedient to You and
would be quick to seek Your forgiveness. Show him the way to worship
You with true enthusiasm and not turn his back on You in any way.

She nagged at him everyday until he couldn't stand it any longer and finally told her his secret. "My hair has never been cut," he confessed, "for I've been a Nazarite to God since before my birth. If my hair were cut, my strength would leave me, and I would become as weak as anyone else."

–Judges 16:16-17 (TLB)

P R A Y E R   F O C U S :
Father, please grant _____ the strength to withstand the temptations of
others to willfully disobey You and Your Word—no matter how insistent
others may be in trying to persuade him to compromise or disobey. Lord,
support _____ so he remains firm in his obedience to You.

ACTION STEPS:

1. Help your young child make a mobile that reflects God's chain of command for the home. Be sure to put God at the top, followed by Dad, Mom, and the children.

2. Have your child write out a list of authorities in his life. Post the list where it's easy to see (or have an older child tuck in to his Bible), and have him pray for a different authority each day.

3. You might read (or have an older child read for themselves) *My Heart Christ's Home* by Robert Boyd Munger.

4. Make several gelatin desserts using heart-shaped molds. Discuss how molds work and how you can change the texture of molds by putting something else into them (fruit or marshmallows). Point out how we change the shape of our lives by putting Christ and His Word in our hearts.

"Prayer is not
conquering God's
reluctance, but
taking hold of
God's willingness."

—PHILLIPS BROOKS

Day 1

Discernment is a reward of persistent search for wisdom and insight.

My child, believe what I say. And remember what I command you. Listen to wisdom. Try with all your heart to gain understanding. Cry out for wisdom. Beg for understanding. Search for it as you would for silver. Hunt for it like hidden treasure. Then you will understand what it means to respect the Lord. Then you will begin to know God. Only the Lord gives wisdom. Knowledge and understanding come from him.

—Proverbs 2:1-6 (NCV)

P R A Y E R   F O C U S :
God help my child, _____ , to listen to wisdom and try with all his heart to gain understanding. Quicken him to listen to what I say and remember what I have asked of him. Lord, lead _____ in earnestly seeking wisdom and understanding. Open his eyes to search for it just as he would for silver or for hidden treasure. Then _____ will understand what it means to respect You, Lord, for only You give wisdom and knowledge and understanding.

"Solid food" is only for the adult, that is, for the man who has developed by experience his power to discriminate between what is good and what is evil.

—Hebrews 5:14 (Phillips)

P R A Y E R   F O C U S :
Dear God, develop discernment in _____ because he has practiced doing what is right again and again. Permit _____ to see and experience the inner victory and confidence that comes from wise discernment.

Day 2

Discernment is using good judgment in our speech and thoughts.

Be wise in the way you act with people who are not believers. Use your time in the best way you can. When you talk, you should always be kind and wise. Then you will be able to answer everyone in the way you should.

—Colossians 4:5-6 (NCV)

PRAYER FOCUS:
God, please entrust to _____ wisdom in the way he acts with people, especially unbelievers. Reveal to him how to use his time wisely. When he speaks, season his speech with kindness and wisdom so he can answer everyone in the way he should.

———————————

Do not be quick with your mouth, do not be hasty in your heart to utter anything before God. God is in heaven and you are on earth, so let your words be few.

—Ecclesiastes 5:2 (NIV)

PRAYER FOCUS:
Dear Lord, guide _____ in how he speaks. Liberate him from being quick to speak and hasty in his heart to say things before You. Cause him to see the wisdom of using discretion in his speech and making his words count for good—even if it means saying less!

Day 3
Discernment leads to making wise choices.

Wisdom and good judgment live together, for wisdom knows where to discover knowledge and understanding. If anyone respects and fears God, he will hate evil. For wisdom hates pride, arrogance, corruption and deceit of every kind.

–Proverbs 8:12-13 (TLB)

P R A Y E R   F O C U S :
Loving Father, teach _____ ways he can demonstrate "wisdom and good judgment living together" in his life. Please help him to know where to discover knowledge and understanding. Lord, I ask that _____ will always respect and fear You and hate what is evil. Also, help him learn to hate the sins of pride and arrogance and corruption.

––––––––––––––

When a wise person sees danger ahead, he avoids it. But a foolish person keeps going and gets into trouble.

–Proverbs 22:3 (NCV)

P R A Y E R   F O C U S :
Merciful God, stand by _____ in all he does so that he becomes wise (discerning) person. Help him to sense when danger is ahead and be determined to avoid it. Keep him, Lord, from being foolish and walking into trouble.

Day 4

Discernment is seeing, understanding, and avoiding a potential evil and its consequences.

A wise man is cautious and turns away from evil, but a fool is arrogant and careless.

—Proverbs 14:16 (NASB)

P R A Y E R   F O C U S :
Merciful heavenly Father, I ask You to give my dear child, _____ , discernment and wisdom. In this world full of subtle evils, may he be sensitive and cautious about his decisions and directions in life!

_____

The prudent sees the evil and hides himself, but the naive go on, and are punished for it.

—Proverbs 22:3 (NASB)

P R A Y E R   F O C U S :
My God, You are the all-seeing One. Open _____ 's eyes to see the evil that lurks for him. Lord, may he actually hide himself from evil and choose to avoid the consequences of indiscretion.

Day 5

Foolishness is the repeated gullibility and indiscretion of the naive.

The simpleton believes every word he hears, but the prudent man looks and considers well where he is going.

–Proverbs 14:15 (AMP)

PRAYER FOCUS:
Wise and discerning God, keep _____ from repeated indiscretion and foolishness. Cause him to learn quickly from his mistakes and not repeat them naively. Give _____ discernment so that he doesn't believe everything he hears.

———————————

As a dog returns to its vomit, so a fool repeats his folly.

–Proverbs 26:11 (NIV)

PRAYER FOCUS:
Father, to repeat a mistake is not good, but to return to a folly is so very foolish. Teach _____ to see through the foolishness of the world's attitudes and actions. Keep him from returning to folly even if "friends" encourage him strongly.

ACTION STEP:

1. To emphasize that discernment senses danger and keeps from walking into trouble, play a blindfold game at home. Choose a family member to be blindfolded. Another family member can be the designated "voice of discernment." Other family members are the "distracting voices of the world."

Set up an obstacle course throughout several rooms in the house by placing cushions, pillows, chairs, etc. in the path. The blindfolded person must listen to the "voice of discernment" to successfully get through the obstacle course. At the same time the "distracting voices" are screaming false directions at the blindfolded person. Have the obstacle course end in the kitchen where the one practicing discretion will be rewarded with a favorite snack.

"*God's pray-ers are societies' best revolutionaries.*"

—DICK EASTMAN

Day 1

Purity is avoiding activities and companions that stir up evil thoughts.

Run from anything that gives you the evil thoughts that young men often have, but stay close to anything that makes you want to do right....enjoy the companionship of those who love the Lord and have pure hearts.

–2 Timothy 2:22   (TLB)

P R A Y E R   F O C U S :
Father, provide _____ the wisdom and strength to flee from anything that would stir up inappropriate desires. Give him a godly desire to have a pure mind and to seek friendship with those who have pure hearts.

_____

I will set before my eyes no vile thing. The deeds of faithless men I hate; they will not cling to me. Men of perverse hearts shall be far from me; I will have nothing to do with evil.

–Psalm 101:3-4 (NIV)

P R A Y E R   F O C U S :
Holy God, I ask that _____ would have a commitment to only look at pure things and to have pure thoughts. Teach him that fantasies arouse feelings that can easily lead to sinful actions. Help him to understand that evil companions stir up evil desires.

Day 2

Purity is yielding to God by withholding our bodies from unbiblical sexual involvement.

For God wants you to be holy and pure, and to keep clear of all sexual sin so that each of you will marry in holiness and honor...

−1 Thessalonians 4:3-4 (TLB)

P R A Y E R   F O C U S :
Father, I ask that You give _____ a desire for a commitment to purity of his sexual life. Put a hedge around him and protect him from the temptations and persuasiveness of his own flesh and our society.

—————————————

Do not let sin control your puny body any longer; do not give in to its sinful desires. Do not let any part of your bodies become tools of wickedness, to be used for sinning;...

−Romans 6:12-13a (TLB)

P R A Y E R   F O C U S :
Lord God, You are the Creator of both passion and purity. I pray that You give _____ self-control over the passions of his life. May his desires not be unbridled. I ask that he does not use any part of his body for impure purposes.

Day 3

Purity of heart is a gift from God.

Create in me a pure heart, O God, and renew a steadfast spirit within me.
—Psalm 51:10 (NIV)

PRAYER FOCUS:
Dear God and Father, I ask that _____ would continually come to You recognizing his need to have a pure heart before You. Take away any waivering in his heart and renew a steadfast spirit within him, so that he can follow You wholeheartedly.

_____

What I am eager for is that all the Christians there will be filled with love that comes from pure hearts, and that their minds will be clean and their faith strong.

—1 Timothy 1:5 (TLB)

PRAYER FOCUS:
Lord, I pray that _____ will be filled with the love that comes from a pure heart and that his mind will be clean and his faith will be strong.

Day 4
Purity is the mark of a true Christian.

Follow God's example in everything you do just as a much loved child imitates his father. Be full of love for others, following the example of Christ who loved you and gave himself to God as a sacrifice to take away your sins. And God was pleased, for Christ's love for you was like a sweet perfume to him. Let there be no sex sin, impurity or greed among you. Let no one be able to accuse you of any such things. Dirty stories, foul talk and coarse jokes—these are not for you. Instead, remind each other of God's goodness and be thankful.

–Ephesians 5:1-4 (TLB)

PRAYER FOCUS:
Loving and faithful Father, help _____ as he faces the temptation to live a life apart from You. Stand by him so he can be strong and follow Your example in everything he does. Lord, give _____ a special love for others—Christ's love—who gave Himself as a sacrifice to take away _____ 's sins. Father, I truly pray that there will be no sexual sin, impurity, or greed in _____ 's life.

Day 5

Immorality should not be practiced even though it is widespread.

...Don't fool yourselves. Those who live immoral lives, who are idol worshipers, adulterers or homosexuals—will have no share in his kingdom....I can do anything I want to if Christ has not said no, but some of these things aren't good for me. Even if I am allowed to do them, I'll refuse to if I think they might get such a grip on me that I can't easily stop when I want to.

–1 Corinthians 6:9b, 12 (TLB)

P R A Y E R   F O C U S :
Lord, permit _____ to recognize immorality for what it is—sin against You. Provide him with great discernment in this area. Give _____ an abundance of courage and steadfastness to turn from anything that would lower his standards or draw him away from doing what You have taught him.

That is why I say to run from sex sin. No other sin affects the body as this one does. When you sin this sin it is against your own body.

–1 Corinthians 6:18 (TLB)

P R A Y E R   F O C U S :
Lord, You tell us that the impact sexual sin has on a person's mind and body is severe. Please protect _____ from ever having to experience the effects of sexual sin. Strengthen his spirit so that he can flee from any situation for potential sexual immorality.

ACTION STEPS:

1. Using 1 Corinthians 6:18 as a basis, explain how the sexually impure person sins against or "bruises" his own body. Then, take a banana that is in the process of ripening and hit it on the outside in several places...as the days progress, peel the banana and note the rotting that has taken place inside. External actions have internal results.

2. Slice the top from a carrot that still has its greens and place it in a pan of water colored with purple food coloring. Watch, daily, as the leaves turn purple. Explain how we also, like the carrot, become on the inside what we are exposed to on the outside.

3. Take a glass jar, and cover the bottom 1 inch with a muddy silt—the silt represents our sexual desires. Fill the rest with clear water. Show your child how impure the water becomes when these desires are inappropriately stirred up...and how long it takes to become pure again.

4. Parents, purity is a crucial area in your child's life. Look for opportunities to reinforce that it is acceptable—even appropriate—to run from temptation. Consider situations your child may face in the future. Verbally enact these, describing ways to respond when facing a particular temptation. While you are in the car is a great time to do this—you have a captive audience!

"Prayer is a strong wall and fortress... it is a goodly Christian weapon."

—MARTIN LUTHER

Day 1

Responsibility is putting aside personal feelings to help meet the needs of another.

"I am the Good Shepherd. The Good Shepherd lays down his life for the sheep.... I am the Good Shepherd and know my own sheep, and they know me,..."

–John 10:11, 14 (TLB)

P R A Y E R   F O C U S :

Father, I want _____ to learn from the example of the Lord Jesus—to be willing to put aside his own feelings to meet the needs of others. Show him that part of being responsible is learning to put other's needs above those of his own.

―――――――――――

Even if we believe that it makes no difference to the Lord whether we do these things, still we cannot just go ahead and do them to please ourselves; for we must bear the "burden" of being considerate of the doubts and fears of others—of those who feel these things are wrong. Let's please the other fellow, not ourselves, and do what is for his good and thus build him up in the Lord.

–Romans 15:1-2 (TLB)

P R A Y E R   F O C U S :

Dear God, I know there will be times when it will be hard for _____ to think of others instead of himself. Please give him a willingness to be considerate of the needs of others. Lord, I pray that _____ would become sensitive and desire to build others up in the Lord—and as a result be truly responsible.

Day 2

Responsibility is the determination to fulfill one's obligations.

"I myself will guarantee his safety; you can hold me personally responsible for him. If I do not bring him back to you and set him here before you, I will bear the blame before you all my life."

–Genesis 43:9 (NIV)

P R A Y E R F O C U S :
Dear God, help _____ understand the importance of taking responsibility in his life. Help him recognize, as Judah did, the opportunities before him and then commit himself to a job with the determination to carry it out. Provide _____ with the discipline and confidence needed to see the task through to completion.

———————

"Now then, please let your servant remain here as my lord's slave in place of the boy, and let the boy return with his brothers. How can I go back to my father if the boy is not with me? No! Do not let me see the misery that would come upon my father."

–Genesis 44:33-34 (NIV)

P R A Y E R F O C U S :
Lord, instill in _____'s heart an understanding of what it means when he fulfills his obligations. When he is asked to take on new responsibilities, give him discernment in his choices. Allow _____ to have the widom to realize that his actions that go along with his responsibilities—good or bad—affect other people.

Day 3

Responsibility is choosing for oneself between right and wrong.

"But if you are unwilling to obey the Lord, then decide today whom you will obey....But as for me and my family, we will serve the Lord."

–Joshua 24:15 (TL

P R A Y E R   F O C U S :

Lord, you are the one true God! My prayer is for _____, that he willingly chooses to be faithful. May _____ be responsible in his choices and always commit himself to serve You.

It was by faith that Moses, when he grew up, refused to be treated as the grandson of the king, but chose to share ill-treatment with God's people instead of enjoying the fleeting pleasures of sin.

–Hebrews 11:24-25 (TLI

P R A Y E R   F O C U S :

Father, like Moses, may my own child, _____, choose to be ill-treated rather than be irresponsible and choose wrongly. Lord, I ask that he would be responsible and proud to be one of Your children and choose not to flirt with sin.

Day 4

**Responsibility is the obligation to use the gifts
and abilities God has given us.**

*As each one has received a special gift, employ it in serving one another, as
good stewards of the manifold grace of God.*

–1 Peter 4:10 (NASB)

P R A Y E R   F O C U S :
Father, You are the Giver of every good and perfect gift. Give me eyes to
see how You have gifted my child, and give _____ the sense of responsibility to use his gifts to glorify You and serve others.

---

*"So you too, when you do all the things which are commanded you, say, 'We
are unworthy slaves; we have done only that which we ought to have done.'"*

–Luke 17:10 (NASB)

P R A Y E R   F O C U S :
Lord, You are the generous Giver. I pray that _____ would follow that
example. Fill him with a joyful spirit in carrying out the responsibilities
for which he is called.

Day 5

Irresponsibility is our laziness that fails to meet the reasonable expectations of God and others.

"And everyone who hears these words of Mine, and does not act upon them, will be like a foolish man, who built his house upon the sand."

—Matthew 7:26 (NASB)

PRAYER FOCUS:
Father, protect _____ from being only a hearer of Your Word. Help him to be a doer of the Word—a young man/woman of action. Deliver _____ from being captured by that spirit of laziness that leads to repeated acts of irresponsibility. Thank You for hearing my prayer.

"And that slave who knew his master's will and did not get ready or act in accord with his will, shall receive many lashes,..."

—Luke 12:47 (NASB)

PRAYER FOCUS:
Lord, keep _____ safe from an "I don't care" attitude. Lift him up to be responsible in preparing and acting according to Your will. Guard _____ from being influenced by others who have been irresponsible in their lives toward You and others.

A C T I O N   S T E P S :

1. Someone has observed that it takes 5-10 positive statements to offset one criticism. Find several specific areas this week in which your child is demonstrating responsibility, and be an encourager.

2. Now is a great time to set up a chart to visibly record the level of responsibility that is being performed by your child in a given area. (See example below.) Concentrate on several areas in which he is doing well and one in which he needs to improve.

"A JOB WELL DONE"

	Teeth	Pets	Bed	Prayers	Home-work	Phone	Room	Trash
Monday								
Tuesday								
Wednesday								
Thursday								
Friday								
Saturday								
Sunday								

COURAGE

"Prayer is not a little habit pinned on to us while we were tied to our mother's apron strings; neither is it a little decent quarter of a minute's grace said over an hour's dinner, but it is a most serious work of our most serious years."

—E.M. BOUNDS

Day 1

Courage is the strength of heart and mind to confront an
opponent with the confidence that I will ultimately succeed.

*Shadrach, Meshach, and Abednego replied, "O Nebuchadnezzar, we are not
worried about what will happen to us. If we are thrown into the flaming
furnace, our God is able to deliver us; and he will deliver us out of your hand,
Your Majesty."*

–Daniel 3:16-17 (TLB)

P R A Y E R   F O C U S :
God, I pray that You will give _____ confidence that You are always
present. Develop in him the assurance that he can courageously trust in
You and not worry about the future.

———————

*You know how badly we had been treated at Philippi just before we came to
you, and how much we suffered there. Yet God gave us the courage to boldly
repeat the same message to you, even though we were surrounded by enemies.*

–1 Thessalonians 2:2 (TLB)

P R A Y E R   F O C U S :
Father, I would ask that You give _____ the authentic courage to be
your witness, although there will be those who ridicule or reject him.

Day 2

Courage is the strength of mind which helps us to face danger without panic.

"Have I not commanded you? Be strong and courageous! Do not tremble or be dismayed, for the Lord your God is with you wherever you go."

–Joshua 1:9 (NASB)

P R A Y E R   F O C U S :

Mighty God who stands strong above every other power in heaven and earth, I pray that You would give _____ a tenacious courage. May he be able to face the dangers of his world (people, places, things) without panic and fear but with strong confidence in You.

_____

Now you don't need to be afraid of the dark anymore, nor fear the dangers of the day; nor dread the plagues of darkness, nor disasters in the morning.

–Psalm 91:5-6 (TLB)

P R A Y E R   F O C U S :

Father, give _____ a radiant courage to face the dark places of his life. Focus his mind on the light and strength of Jesus Christ. Remove all panic from _____ that he may know You are always present and caring for him.

Day 3

Courage is standing firm when facing adverse circumstances.

"And now, compelled by the Spirit, I am going to Jerusalem, not knowing what will happen to me there. I only know that in every city the Holy Spirit warns me that prison and hardships are facing me. However, I consider my life worth nothing to me, if only I may finish the race and complete the task the Lord Jesus has given me—the task of testifying to the gospel of God's grace."

–Acts 20:22-24 (NIV)

P R A Y E R   F O C U S :
Merciful Father, I lift _____ before You and pray that he be willing to go wherever You lead. I pray that he sets his heart on following You at any cost. When finding himself in a difficult place, give him courage and confidence in You alone. Lord, strengthen _____ to run the race and complete the task You have planned for him. I want him to be able to talk about the evidence of Your grace in his life.

———————————

"Be strong and courageous. Do not be afraid or terrified because of them, for the Lord your God goes with you; He will never leave you nor forsake you."

–Deuteronomy 31:6 (NIV)

P R A Y E R   F O C U S :
Dear God, build up _____ to become a person who is strong and courageous because of his trust in You. As he faces people or circumstances that will test his convictions, help him to not be paralyzed because of them, but always remember that You are with him.

Day 4

Courage is putting confidence in God ahead of loyalty to others.

(Read verses 5-9.) Now when Daniel learned that the decree had been published, he went home to his upstairs room where the windows opened toward Jerusalem. Three times a day he got down on his knees and prayed, giving thanks to his God, just as he had done before. Then these men went as a group and found Daniel praying and asking God for help.

–Daniel 6:10-11 (NIV)

P R A Y E R   F O C U S :

Lord God, my child will face many situations that will test his faith in You. Give him the courage to keep his eyes fixed on You. I pray that his commitment to You becomes stronger than any other loyalty in his life. God, develop in _____ the character of Daniel—a loyal friend whose loyalty to You was unsurpassed.

Day 5

When fear controls us and our faith is small, the courageous person calls to Jesus, Who is always there to rescue us.

...So Peter went over the side of the boat and walked on the water toward Jesus. But when he looked around at the high waves, he was terrified and began to sink. "Save me, Lord!" he shouted. Instantly Jesus reached out His hand and rescued him. "O man of little faith," Jesus said. "Why did you doubt me?"

–Matthew 14:29b-31 (TLB)

P R A Y E R   F O C U S :
Loving Father, give _____ grace when he finds himself overtaken by fear. Lord, there are so many things in life that could cause him to live in fear. Help keep his eyes on Jesus when he finds himself surrounded by the "high waves" of life. I pray that he learns to turn to the Lord Jesus in his fear and finds that Jesus Christ is always sufficient.

But soon a terrible storm arose. High waves began to break into the boat until it was nearly full of water and about to sink. Jesus was asleep at the back of the boat with his head on a cushion. Frantically they wakened him, shouting, "Teacher, don't you even care that we are all about to drown?" Then he rebuked the wind and said to the sea, "Quiet down!" And the wind fell, and there was a great calm! And he asked them, "Why were you so fearful? Don't you even yet have confidence in me?"

–Mark 4:37-40 (TLB)

P R A Y E R   F O C U S :
Lord, when fear overtakes _____ , help him to remember that You can calm the fears of his heart as well as the waves of the sea. In the fearful things of _____ 's life, show him the way to place himself in Your sovereign control.

A C T I O N   S T E P S :

1. Sit down with your child and discuss the possible struggles in his life. To help younger children understand this concept, flip through a contemporary news magazine and tear out pictures of things that might frighten your child. Discuss how Jesus can give us the courage to face our fears with confidence.

2. Take advantage of opportunities while riding in the car to present hypothetical situations to your child that would require courage on his part. Possible topics could be drugs, alcohol, vandalism, sex, cheating, etc. For example: "Suppose you and your friends were out one night and someone began to pass around drugs. What would you do when the drugs came to you? What would you do if your friends wouldn't leave you alone?"

3. Read Daniel 6 to your children in the Living Bible, if possible. Talk about the different people and what they did. Especially point out how courageous Daniel was. Parents, children love to act out plays for you. Let them use Daniel 6 as their script and put on a play about "the courage of Daniel."

4. To encourage means "to put courage in." Have a mealtime rally where each person takes an opportunity to tell what he or she appreciates about another family member. Focus on one person at a time, and everyone must share something...positive!

"There is nothing that makes us love man so much as praying for him."

—WILLIAM LAW

Day 1

Servanthood is sacrificing one's own privileges and liberties for the good of another.

We should be willing to be both vegetarians and teetotallers or abstain from anything else if by doing otherwise we should impede a brother's progress in the faith.

—Romans 14:21 (Phillips)

P R A Y E R   F O C U S :
Lord God, Your Son came as a servant of men. Instill within _____ 's heart a desire to become a servant to those around him. Help him be willing to give up any freedom to help another person grow in faith.

_____

Don't think only of yourself. Try to think of the other fellow, too, and what is best for him.

–1 Corinthians 10:24 (TLB)

P R A Y E R   F O C U S :
Father, it is so hard to think of the other person first—or at all. Being a servant sounds nice, but it takes effort. Give _____ a willingness to become the kind of servant that doesn't mind putting out the effort and looks out for the good of the other person!

Day 2

Servanthood is a cure for selfishness.

When you do things, do not let selfishness or pride be your guide. Be humble and give more honor to others than to yourselves. Do not be interested only in your own life, but be interested in the lives of others.

–Philippians 2:3-4 (NCV)

PRAYER FOCUS:
Lord God, I pray that You would work in _____ 's life. I don't want selfishness or pride to control him. Teach him to be humble and honor others more than himself. Lord, give _____ an interest in being involved in the lives of other people.

———————————

No one should try to do what will help only himself. He should try to do what is good for others.

–1 Corinthians 10:24 (NCV)

PRAYER FOCUS:
Father, open _____ 's eyes to see the need to reach out to those around him with a servant's heart. Give _____ the willingness that always wants to try to do what is good for others.

Day 3

Servanthood keeps us aware of another's needs.

"He who serves you as a servant is the greatest among you. Whoever makes himself great will be made humble. Whoever makes himself humble will be made great."

–Matthew 23:11-12 (NCV)

P R A Y E R   F O C U S :
Lord, help _____ take the first step in seeing that, in Your eyes, the one who is willing to serve is greatest. God, work in _____ 's life, that he will learn to recognize the needs of others and allow You to use him in meeting those needs.

"But among you it is quite different. Anyone wanting to be a leader among you must be your servant. And if you want to be right at the top, you must serve like a slave. Your attitude must be like my own, for I, the Messiah, did not come to be served, but to serve, and to give my life as a ransom for many."

–Matthew 20:26-28 (TLB)

P R A Y E R   F O C U S :
Father, teach _____ the ways of leadership that You desire—to have a purpose of being a willing servant and putting the needs of others above those of his own. Develop in _____ the same attitude as Your Son, Jesus, Who didn't come to be served but to serve.

Day 4

Servanthood is spiritual greatness through humility and servitude.

So Jesus called them to him and said, "As you know, the kings and great men of the earth lord it over the people; but among you it is different. Whoever wants to be great among you must be your servant. And whoever wants to be greatest of all must be the slave of all. For even I, the Messiah, am not here to be served, but to help others, and to give my life a ransom for many."

–Mark 10:42-45 (TLB)

P R A Y E R   F O C U S :
Most loving God, I thank You that Your Son was willing to be a Servant to man. I thank You for the example He gave us of serving others. Help _____ to develop a heart for serving others as he learns of Christ's example. Lord, help _____ choose to demonstrate a servant's heart.

———————————

For though I am free from all men, I have made myself a slave to all, that I might win the more.

–1 Corinthians 9:19 (NASB)

P R A Y E R   F O C U S :
Almighty God, I ask that You lead _____ to be a servant of all men that he might draw them to You. I pray that he willingly undertakes this humble service, and by doing so, he will experience true spiritual greatness.

Day 5

Self-interest is providing for oneself at the expense of others—putting one's personal desires above the needs of others.

"... for I was hungry, and you gave Me nothing to eat; I was thirsty, and you gave Me nothing to drink; I was a stranger, and you did not invite Me in; naked, and you did not clothe Me..."

–Matthew 25:42-43a (NASB)

P R A Y E R   F O C U S :
Father, deliver _____ from this great weakness of the flesh—selfishness! Help him to become a servant to others. Help him to become sensitive to the physical and emotional needs of those around him.

_____

People curse the man who holds his grain for higher prices, but they bless the man who sells it to them in their time of need.

–Proverbs 11:26 (TLB)

P R A Y E R   F O C U S :
Lord Jesus, keep _____ from seeking his own self-interest. Fill his heart with the desire that doesn't look out for his own needs at the expense of others. Show _____ ways he can demonstrate servanthood by having a generous, sharing spirit.

A C T I O N   S T E P S :

1. Spend some time as a family learning to become aware of the "everyday" needs of one another by "walking in someone else's shoes." Blindfold one person at a time and have them step into another family member's shoes. As the blindfolded person walks around the room, he must determine in whose steps he is walking. He can do this by the feel of the shoes and by thinking of the likes and responsibilities of that person. Before you remove the blindfold, he must tell how he will meet a practical need of the person whose shoes he is wearing.

2. Plan to have a "servanthood meal." The main goal is to have your family members identify and respond to the needs of others. Prepare the needed number of places to serve your family in the following way:

One plate: Large double portions of the entire meal, including drink and dessert.
One (or more) plates: A small portion of everything— without dessert.
One (or more) plates: Bread and water.
One plate: Nothing.

Arrange the plates on your countertop allowing family members to serve themselves— "first come, first served." Let the meal continue until those with an abundance see the need to share and take responsible actions to do so. By way of application, you can also draw a comparison between recognizing and meeting the needs within your family and the needs of all people worldwide.

CONTENTMENT

*"One may lack talent
for doing great things,
as men count greatness,
but one's station in life
does not determine
greatness in the sight of
God. He looks for
dedicated hearts
carrying prayerful
burdens. God longs
for those who work
at prayer."*

—DICK EASTMAN

Day 1

Contentment is realizing that God can provide an inner peace and tranquillity regardless of circumstances.

The Lord is good to those who wait for Him, to the person who seeks Him. It is good that he waits silently for the salvation of the Lord.

           –Lamentations 3:25-26 (NASB)

P R A Y E R F O C U S :
Father, give _____ the ability to see that You give Your best to those who wait on You. I ask, Lord, that _____ would possess a genuine contentment with himself as a person, as well as the circumstances he faces each day.

I would have despaired unless I had believed that I would see the goodness of the Lord in the land of the living. Wait for the Lord; be strong, and let your heart take courage; yes, wait for the Lord.

           –Psalm 27:13-14 (NASB)

P R A Y E R F O C U S :
Lord, teach _____ to have that contentment that hopes in You. Give him the assurance that leads to inner peace, tranquility, and contentment.

Day 2

Genuine contentment finds its foundation in a quiet trust in the Lord.

My heart is not proud, O Lord, my eyes are not haughty; I do not concern myself with great matters or things too wonderful for me. But I have stilled and quieted my soul; like a weaned child with its mother, like a weaned child is my soul within me.

—Psalm 131:1-2 (NIV)

P R A Y E R   F O C U S :
Merciful God, instill in the life of my child a heart that is not proud and eyes that are not haughty. Help _____ in being able to place the concerns of his life confidently in Your care. I pray that my child would be favorable in Your eyes. Lord, give him a spirit that is still and quiet before You.

———————

Be delighted with the Lord. Then he will give you all your heart's desires. Commit everything you do to the Lord. Trust him to help you do it and he will.

—Psalm 37:4-5 (TLB)

P R A Y E R   F O C U S :
Lord, You alone are our true contentment. Help _____ to understand that gaining genuine contentment comes as he learns to delight himself in knowing You. Help _____ see that as he commits himself to You in quiet trust, he will experience real contentment.

Day 3

Contentment comes in understanding that it is God who supplies our needs.

And my God will meet all your needs according to His glorious riches in Christ Jesus.

–Philippians 4:19 (NIV)

PRAYER FOCUS:
Loving God, comfort _____ when he is hurting. Sustain him with Your grace so he remembers that You will meet his needs. As _____ learns to depend on You in this way, help him to experience true contentment.

———————

God is able to make it up to you by giving you everything you need and more, so that there will not only be enough for your own needs, but plenty left over to give joyfully to others.

–2 Corinthians 9:8 (TLB)

PRAYER FOCUS:
Father, I thank You for the many ways You have blessed and provided for _____. Confirm in his heart all that You have done. Show him that You have given him even more than he's asked for. Allow him to see ways that he can share his abundance with others.

Day 4

Contentment is the result of responding to Christ in joyful obedience.

Not that I was ever in need, for I have learned how to get along happily whether I have much or little. I know how to live on almost nothing or with everything. I have learned the secret of contentment in every situation, whether it be a full stomach or hunger, plenty or want; for I can do everything God asks me to with the help of Christ who gives me the strength and power.

–Philippians 4:11-13 (TLB)

PRAYER FOCUS:
Dear Lord, our society doesn't understand the meaning of contentment very well. It's going to be hard for _____ to battle the influences of greed all around him. Show him that the way to true contentment in life comes not from having all he wants, but through joyful obedience to Christ. Help him to understand that he can do everything You ask of him with Christ's help.

But he said to me, "My grace is sufficient for you, for my power is made perfect in weakness." Therefore I will boast all the more gladly about my weaknesses, so that Christ's power may rest on me. That is why, for Christ's sake, I delight in weaknesses, in insults, in hardships, in persecutions, in difficulties. For when I am weak, then I am strong.

–2 Corinthians 12:9-10 (NIV)

PRAYER FOCUS:
Father, You alone are all-sufficient for all of our needs. I ask that Your Holy Spirit gives _____ an understanding heart in this area. Help him to know that You are sufficient for him, even in his greatest weaknesses and struggles. Help _____ to see he can be joyfully content wherever he finds himself, knowing that, in You, when he is weak, then he is strong.

Day 5

Covetousness is the loss of contentment that leads to the
greed and envy of the unrighteous.

*Rest in the Lord and wait patiently for Him; do not fret because of him who
prospers in his way, because of the man who carries out wicked schemes.*

—Psalm 37:7 (NASB)

PRAYER FOCUS:
Father, give _____ victory over any spirit of covetousness. Keep
_____ from becoming greedy or envious of those whose goal in life is
to acquire position or possessions.

---

*But people who long to be rich soon begin to do all kinds of wrong things to
get money, things that hurt them and make them evil-minded and finally
send them to hell itself.*

—1 Timothy 6:9 (TLB)

PRAYER FOCUS:
Lord, You want to provide our every need. Help _____ find
contentment in You alone. Take away from him any love of money.
Show _____ how to see money as a means to honor You.

ACTION STEPS:

1. Begin a new family tradition—create a "blessing book." Use this book regularly or on special occasions (birthdays, Thanksgiving, etc.) to remember all the ways God has met your needs as a family.

2. Agree on a special outside place that you all enjoy. Go there and share times when you have had to "wait on the Lord." Discuss how this teaches contentment.

3. As a family, be transparent about the honest desires of your heart (your goals, dreams, and ambitions). Then, using Psalm 37:4-5, talk about the struggles or any confusion you have felt in trying to understand what it means to delight yourself in the Lord, the One who fulfills the true desires of our hearts.

"God only comes to those who ask Him to come; and He cannot refuse to come to those who implore Him long, often, and ardently."

—SIMONE WEIL

Day 1

Endurance requires a lifestyle built on trusting God and being obedient to Him.

This calls for patient endurance on the part of the saints who obey God's commandments and remain faithful to Jesus.

–Revelation 14:12 (NIV)

P R A Y E R   F O C U S :
Dear God, may Your Holy Spirit encourage _____ to begin building a lifestyle of patient endurance. Instill in _____ a willingness to obey Your commandments and always be faithful to Jesus Christ. Deepen his trust in You as his God and Savior.

Then Nebuchadnezzar said, "Praise be to the God of Shadrach, Meshach and Abednego, who has sent his angel and rescued his servants! They trusted in him and defiled the king's command and were willing to give up their lives rather than serve or worship any god except their own God."

–Daniel 3:28 (NIV)

P R A Y E R   F O C U S :
Lord, how I pray that my child might develop a heart of endurance like that of these young men, Shadrach, Meshach, and Abednego. Give _____ the strength he needs to be able to stand firm when facing adversity. Help him to say, "I serve God, and He is able to save me from any situation. But even if He doesn't, I will not disobey Him; I will do what I know is right in His sight."

Day 2

Endurance is the capacity to bear up under difficult—unpleasant, painful, stressful—circumstances in a Christ-like manner.

Blessed is the man who perseveres under trial, because when he has stood the test, he will receive the crown of life that God has promised to those who love him.

—James 1:12 (NIV)

PRAYER FOCUS:
Father, thank You that You will never leave us or forsake us. As _____ faces difficult situations, remind him of this truth. Strengthen him to be able to endure these trials so that one day he can receive the crown of life You promised to those who love You.

For it is commendable if a man bears up under the pain of unjust suffering because he is conscious of God. But how is it to your credit if you receive a beating for doing wrong and endure it? But if you suffer for doing good and you endure it, this is commendable before God.

—1 Peter 2:19-20 (NIV)

PRAYER FOCUS:
Father, there are so many difficult things my child must face in these days. I ask that _____ will be a young person who will have the strength and courage to stand up under these pressures because he is striving to live for You. Allow _____ to recognize that he might have to suffer for doing what he knows is right, but that through his endurance, his actions will be pleasing to You.

Day 3

Endurance is essential to faith.

"But those enduring to the end shall be saved."

–Matthew 24:13 (TLB)

P R A Y E R   F O C U S :
Father, I know that as a believer in Jesus Christ, my child will have to expect and face persecution for his faith. Please sustain him with Your presence. Supply _____ with the endurance he needs to stand firm against all opposition.

"And everyone will hate you because you are mine. But all who endure to the end without renouncing me shall be saved."

–Mark 13:13 (TLB)

P R A Y E R   F O C U S :
Dear God, when _____'s faith is challenged, stand by him as he learns to endure these attacks. I pray that he becomes even stronger in his faith in You.

Day 4

Endurance is the patient, committed pursuit of those things pleasing to God.

And let us not get tired of doing what is right, for after a while we will reap a harvest of blessing if we don't get discouraged and give up.
—Galatians 6:9   (TLB)

P R A Y E R   F O C U S :
Father, I pray that You gently build endurance into _____'s life. Give _____ a heart that helps him to keep on pressing on.

Therefore, since we are surrounded by such a great cloud of witnesses, let us throw off everything that hinders and the sin that so easily entangles, and let us run with perseverance the race marked out for us.
—Hebrews 12:1   (NIV)

P R A Y E R   F O C U S :
Lord, You have sovereignly marked our path. I ask that You enable _____ to run the race of life with great endurance. Keep _____ from being tripped up, distracted, or losing heart in the race. Help him to keep his eyes on You.

Day 5

Giving up can cause guilt and disappointment which takes our focus off of the Lord.

No temptation has overtaken you but such as is common to man; and God is faithful, who will not allow you to be tempted beyond what you are able, but with the temptation will provide the way of escape also, that you may be able to endure it.

–1 Corinthians 10:13 (NASB)

P R A Y E R   F O C U S :
Lord, give _____ the endurance to stand against every temptation.
Deliver _____ from ever giving up on looking to You for strength, wisdom, and encouragement.

For you have need of endurance, so that when you have done the will of God, you may receive what is promised....But My righteous one shall live by faith; and if he shrinks back, My soul has no pleasure in him. But we are not of those who shrink back to destruction, but of those who have faith to the preserving of the soul.

–Hebrews 10:36, 38-39 (NASB)

P R A Y E R   F O C U S :
Father, please give _____ a spirit of endurance. Build him up that he will not shrink back from a life of faith. Encourage him to not give up when he encounters people or ideas that will test his faith. I want _____ to have the kind of faith that is preserving to his soul.

A C T I O N   S T E P :

1. To show how Christians sometimes must endure
persecution for their beliefs, set a mock trial in your home.
Designate someone to be judge, prosecutor, defendant,
and defense counselor. Let the judge read the charges
being brought against the defendant. Some examples of
possible charges are:

(1) you believe God created this world
(2) you believe that the Lord is a personal God
(3) you believe Jesus Christ was God
(4) you don't lie or cheat to get your own way
(5) you avoid drugs, alcohol, and sex

Allow the prosecutor and defense counselor to take turns
questioning and informing the witness as to the truth of the
charges. Look up the following verses to see how one might
biblically answer the charges. Note: the following verses
correspond, one through five, to the charges above.

(1) Genesis 1-2; Psalm 19:1; Psalm 8:1-3; Romans 1:20
(2) Psalm 139; Jeremiah 9:24
(3) Colossians 1:15-17; John 1:1-2, 14
(4) Psalm 101:1-3; Psalm 15; Proverbs 6:16-19
(5) 1 Corinthians 6:18-20; Proverbs 23:26-32;
    Proverbs 7:6-27

Gary C. Harrell

Gary Harrell is co-pastor of Fellowship Bible Church of Northwest Arkansas. He has been married more than 25 years to his high school sweetheart, Anne. He is the father of two girls, Heidi and Holli.

Gary graduated from the University of Arkansas in 1970 with a degree in business administration. He immediately joined the staff of Campus Crusade for Christ where he served on the University of Tennessee (Knoxville) campus. Gary holds graduate degrees from Dallas Theological Seminary and Southwestern Baptist Theological Seminary. Gary has served as dean of students at Dallas Bible College and as associate pastor of University Baptist Church, Fayetteville, Ark. In 1988, he became a teaching pastor at Fellowship Bible Church of Northwest Arkansas, where he presently serves as pastor of small-group ministries. Currently, Gary is working on his doctorate of ministry degree at Fuller Theological Seminary in California.

Anne Arkins

Anne Arkins is a mother of four grown children, as well as a grandmother, writer, and Bible study teacher in Bentonville, Ark., where she attends Fellowship Bible Church of Northwest Arkansas. She has a degree in secondary education from the University of Arkansas. Anne has written and taught women's Bible study material and is involved in mentoring young women. Along with her physician husband, Jim, she speaks at FamilyLife Conferences across the country.

Take a
Weekend
to Raise Your
Children
for a Lifetime!

Parenting. It is one of the most important responsibilities we have, and yet most of us receive little training.

In one weekend, the FamilyLife Parenting Conference will equip you with the principles and tools you need to be a more effective parent for a lifetime.

Whether you're just getting started or in the turbulent years of adolescence, we'll show you the biblical blueprints for raising your children. You'll hear from dynamic speakers and actually leave the conference with a written plan tailored for your child. You'll receive proven effective principles from parents just like you who have dedicated their lives to helping families.

YOU'LL LEARN HOW TO:
- Build a strong relationship with your child
- Help your child develop an emotional, spiritual, and sexual identity
- Develop moral character in your child
- Give your child a sense of mission
- Pass on your values to your child

FAMILYLIFE PARENTING CONFERENCE
To register or receive a free brochure and schedule, call FamilyLife at
1-800-FL-TODAY.

FAMILYLIFE™
Bringing Timeless Principles Home

AUDIO RESOURCES FOR YOUR FAMILY

"BEYOND ABSTINENCE: HELPING YOUR TEEN STAY PURE"

with Dennis and Barbara Rainey

This groundbreaking series helps parents to openly and honestly discuss sex with their teens. The Raineys challenge parents to go beyond teaching abstinence as the goal of sex education, making strong moral values and character the end result. Help your teen gain a godly view of his sexuality, and equip him to properly handle the temptations he'll face. (5 audio cassettes) (#32337). $19.95

"A FOUNDATION FOR MORAL PURITY: TEACHING YOUR CHILDREN ABOUT SEXUALITY"

with Dennis and Barbara Rainey

It's never too early to begin building a foundation for godly, responsible sexual behavior in your children. In this informative audio series, the Raineys present a comprehensive plan for teaching children about sex from a solid biblical approach. Help your children develop moral excellence, sound character, and the ability to make the right choices. (4 audio cassettes)(#32336)..$19.95

"HOW CHILDREN COME TO FAITH IN CHRIST"

by Dennis Rainey with guest Jim Elliff

Most Christian parents have no greater desire than to see their child come to faith in Christ. This insightful audio series helps parents lead their child to faith in Christ in a way that is relevant to his age and stage in life and then, encourage that faith in creative, memorable ways.

(3 audio cassettes) (#32327) $14.95

"A BIBLICAL APPROACH TO SPANKING"

by Dennis and Barbara Rainey

In a society where spanking and child abuse are considered synonymous, should parents spank their children? Dennis and Barbara show how proper discipline is both biblical and beneficial for your child. Learn the "do's and don'ts" of spanking and how to use spanking to build character in your child.

(5 audio cassettes) (#31084)...................$24.95

Call 1-800-FL-TODAY
for these great resources for your family!
PRICES ARE SUBJECT TO CHANGE